# JAPAN
## the land

Bobbie Kalman

### The Lands, Peoples, and Cultures Series

Toronto
New York · Crabtree Publishing Company

## The Lands, Peoples, and Cultures Series

Created by Bobbie Kalman

**Writing team**
Bobbie Kalman
Janine Schaub
Christine Arthurs

**Editor-in-Chief**
Bobbie Kalman

**Editors**
Janine Schaub
Christine Arthurs
Margaret Hoogeveen
Christine McClymont

**Research**
Moira Daly
Virginia Neale

**Design and layout**
Heather Delfino
Margaret Hoogeveen

**Printer**
Worzalla Publishing Company
Stevens Point, Wisconsin

**Illustrations**
John Mantha p. 6, 13.

**Photography acknowledgments**
Cover: Al Harvey/Masterfile
Carol Baum: p. 9(top); Ian Clifford/E-Side Studios: p. 31(top right), 31(bottom);
Courtesy of Japan Information Centre: p. 7(top), 8(bottom right), 21, 24;
Courtesy of Japan National Tourist Organization: p. 8(bottom left), 9(bottom), 11,
12, 18, 19, 20-21, 23(top, bottom right), 28, 29; Margus Jukkum: p. 7(bottom);
Gayle McDougall: p. 15, 31(center); Royal Ontario Museum: p. 14;
Robert Sischy: p. 16(bottom), 22-23, 25, 30; Tom Skudra: p. 4-5, 27(right);
Tony Stone/Masterfile: Title page, p. 8(top), 26-27; Tokyo National Museum: p. 10;
Elias Wakan/Pacific Rim Slide Bank: p. 16(top), 17, 21(right inset), 30(top left).

## For Marc

**Cataloguing in Publication Data**

Kalman, Bobbie, 1947-
  Japan, the land

(Lands, peoples, and cultures series)
Includes index.

ISBN 0-86505-204-2 (bound) ISBN 0-86505-284-0 (pbk.)
1. Japan - Description and travel - Juvenile literature.
2. Japan - History - Juvenile literature.
I. Kalman, Bobbie, 1947-   II. Series.

DS806.J3   1989        j952        LC 93-6162

**Published by**
Crabtree Publishing Company

| 350 Fifth Avenue | 360 York Road, RR 4 | 73 Lime Walk |
| Suite 3308 | Niagara-on-the-Lake | Headington |
| New York | Ontario, Canada | Oxford OX3 7AD |
| N.Y. 10118 | L0S 1J0 | United Kingdom |

# Contents

Thousands of years ago the Chinese saw the sun rise over the islands to the east and named this country *jih-pen*. *Jih-pen* means "the source of the sun." This land came to be known as Japan by the English-speaking world, but the Japanese call it *Nippon*. The sun is an important symbol for the Japanese. It is represented by the big, red ball in the center of their national flag.

The early Japanese who emigrated from far and wide were thankful for having found their beautiful new home. Japan's gentle seasons, fertile soil, and breathtaking scenery must have seemed like gifts from the heavens to these early settlers.

Although most of Japan's 121 million people now live in crowded cities, they still love nature just as their ancestors did. Modern-day Japanese make regular outings to enjoy the lush beauty of the countryside. Bamboo forests, fast-flowing rivers, and picturesque coastlines are just a few of nature's gifts to the land of Japan.

# A land of many islands

Japan is a long, narrow string of islands over three thousand kilometers long and four hundred kilometers at its widest point. No matter where you travel in Japan, the seashore is never far away. It is hard to believe, but this small country is made up of more than 3900 islands! Most of Japan's population lives on the four main islands of Honshu, Shikoku, Kyushu, and Hokkaido.

## Mountainous interiors

Almost three quarters of Japan's land area is covered by mountains! The bases of the mountains along the coast provide the only flat land in the country. Cities, industries, and farms must share this small area. Almost half of the huge population is crowded onto a thin strip of land that is less than three percent of Japan's total area! This strip of land runs along the coastline of Honshu, Japan's largest island.

## *Fujisan*

When the sky is clear in Japan, you can always see a mountain in the distance! The island of Honshu is the home of Japan's highest mountains. The Japanese Alps run through Honshu's center, with many huge peaks reaching heights of over three thousand meters. Taller still is Mount Fuji, a volcano that is 3776 meters high. This majestic mountain, which the Japanese call *Fujisan,* is about a hundred kilometers from Tokyo.

*Japan's closest neighbors are China, Korea, and the U.S.S.R.*

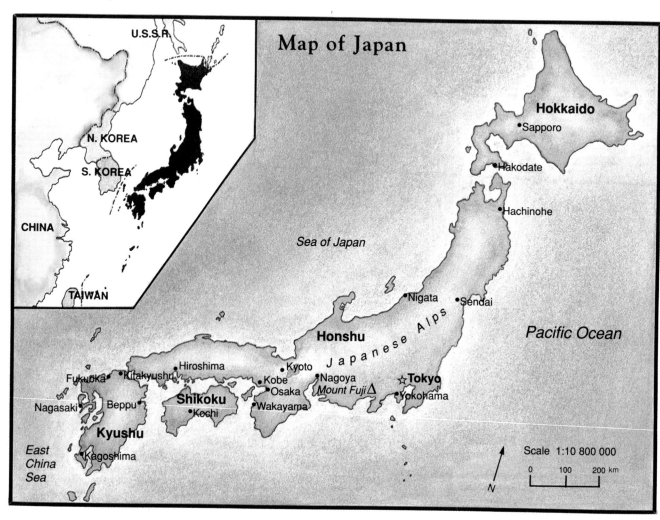

## Early blossoms

The central region of Japan is mild for most of the year, but temperatures in the far northern and southern areas of the country vary greatly. In January, village streets on the island of Hokkaido and in the northwestern part of Honshu are often buried under several meters of snow. At the same time of year, flowers bloom in the southern regions of Kyushu.

## Lots of rain

Between 100 and 300 centimeters of rain fall on Japan every year! This means that many kinds of trees, plants, and flowers flourish throughout the country. The rainy season starts in the south and works its way north. It lasts from early June to mid-July, followed by very hot, humid weather.

*Most Japanese climb Mount Fuji at least once. It takes between five and nine hours to reach the top.*

*Japan's countryside is lush, green, and picturesque.*

*Although the climate of Japan is mild, the northern regions receive plenty of snow.*

*Almost three quarters of Japan's people live in busy, congested cities. The most crowded of all is Tokyo.*

*(left) Japanese farms produce three quarters of the nation's food by using modern machines and efficient methods.*

*Even the most natural-looking gardens in Japan have been carefully planned to capture the fragile beauty of nature.*

*Some of Japan's 4000 islands are just rocks that stick up above the water line.*

# Winds, earthquakes, and giant waves

At the end of summer in Japan huge storms that resemble hurricanes start forming. These storms are called typhoons. Typhoon is a Chinese word meaning "great wind." Typhoons are so strong that they can blow down trees and topple buildings. They often cause floods and landslides in the coastal areas. When a typhoon warning is announced over the radio, everyone goes home immediately. The streets empty, and traffic stops. It is important to be in a protected place indoors when a typhoon strikes. After a typhoon has occurred, communities must spend large sums of money repairing and rebuilding.

## Shifting plates

Typhoons are not the only danger to Japan. Japan is located on an unstable area of the earth's surface. The earth's crust is not one smooth layer like an eggshell. It is made up of several big pieces called plates. These plates constantly move at very slow speeds. Some are moving towards one another, and others are moving apart. Japan is located near the edge of a plate. The movement of this plate causes natural phenomena such as earthquakes, volcanoes, and giant waves.

## Earthquake drills

The Japanese are concerned that the next big earthquake might be even more disastrous than the one in 1923 because there are now more people and buildings in Japan. Although nothing can be done to prevent an earthquake, people can prepare for one. Japanese buildings are constructed to absorb the shock of large tremors. Office workers and school children have regular earthquake drills. During these drills people turn off their gas stoves and electric heaters to prevent fires. They then find shelter under a table or in a doorway. Many homes have earthquake survival kits containing food and medicine.

## Giant waves

Earthquakes can start on land or at sea. When an earthquake occurs under the sea, it sometimes creates *tsunami*. *Tsunami* are massive waves that can be as tall as giant ferris wheels! As the huge walls of water slam against the shore, they bring flooding and widespread destruction. In 1703 at Awa, Japan, one *tsunami* killed over a hundred thousand people! At one time *tsunami* were mistakenly called tidal waves, but they have no connection with tides.

## Hot springs

The same movement of the earth's plates that causes earthquakes also creates hot springs. Hot springs, called *onsen*, are natural pools filled with water heated deep inside the earth. Unlike earthquakes, hot springs are a source of great pleasure and entertainment. One of the most popular bathing spots in Japan is a hot-spring spa in the small city of Beppu. Millions of people visit Beppu each year to relax in its steamy pools and admire its lush forest scenery.

*(inset) A group of school children visit a hot spring.*

*This famous Japanese painting shows a dreaded* tsunami.

## A dangerous dragon

An old legend describes the islands of Japan as the back of a huge, sleeping sea dragon. Whenever the dragon stirs in its sleep, it causes an earthquake. The most devastating earthquake in Japan's history happened on September 1, 1923. It left the cities of Tokyo and Yokohama in ruins and resulted in over a hundred thousand deaths. The quake struck at noon, just as people were lighting fires on which they would prepare their lunches. Most of the damage was caused by these fires, which spread quickly throughout the cities.

#  Volcanoes

Many of Japan's mountains were formed by volcanoes. When the plates of the earth move, melted rock, called magma, is forced up from inside the earth through weak spots in the earth's crust. These spots can be long pipes or simply cracks in the ground. Magma shoots out with a roar or oozes out like hot jam. After it has come in contact with air, it is called lava. Lava burns everything in its path. When lava finally cools down, it hardens into rock. After a volcano has erupted many times, the layers of hardened lava eventually build up to form a mountain.

## Active volcanoes

Volcanoes that erupt from time to time are called active volcanoes. An active volcano can mean disaster for nearby communities. Along with burning lava, an eruption also sends out clouds of black smoke, gases, and sometimes enough ash to bury entire buildings. The people who live close to active volcanoes must be ready to flee at a moment's notice! Ten percent of the world's active volcanoes—sixty-seven in all—are found in Japan.

## Volcanoes that do not erupt

Most of Japan's volcanoes are not active. Old volcanoes that have not erupted for a long time, but still might erupt, are called dormant volcanoes. Mount Fuji, the most famous of Japan's two hundred volcanoes, is a dormant volcano. If a volcano has not erupted for thousands of years, then it is called extinct.

## Volcano facts

- When a volcano is about to erupt, the earth trembles. These small rumblings are caused by magma squeezing through cracks inside the ground.
- Lava can flow as fast as a river or creep along at a snail's pace.
- A volcano sometimes lets off gases that smell like rotten eggs!
- A volcano can spew a fiery fountain into the sky that is as high as the CN Tower in Toronto, Canada. This tower is the world's tallest free-standing structure and is over 550 meters tall!
- Clouds of smoke, steam, and ash from a large volcano cause beautiful sunsets!

*(opposite page) Some active volcanoes constantly spew out smoke and gases.*

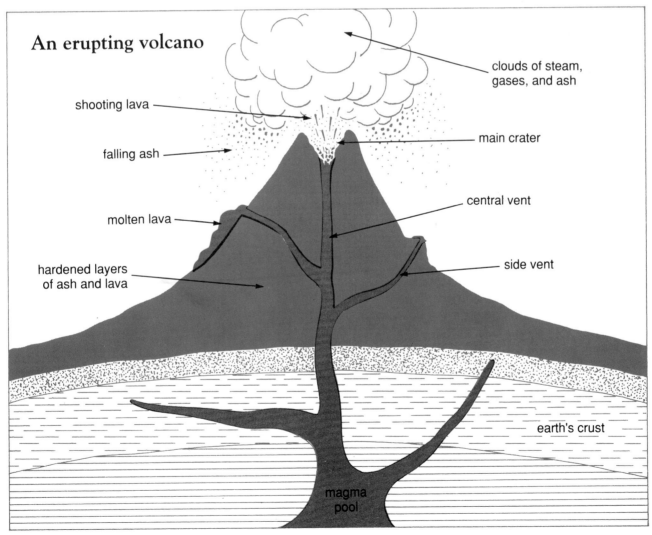

**An erupting volcano**

- clouds of steam, gases, and ash
- shooting lava
- main crater
- falling ash
- central vent
- molten lava
- side vent
- hardened layers of ash and lava
- earth's crust
- magma pool

# The early days of Japan

## The Ainu
The first group of people to live in Japan were the Ainu. The Ainu are quite different in appearance from the Japanese. Their eyes are rounded, and they have more body hair and paler skin than most Japanese. There are a few thousand Ainu left in Japan, but only around three hundred are of full Ainu ancestry. These original people now live in the northern part of Japan on the island of Hokkaido.

## Asian influences
The Japanese are not descendants of the Ainu. They are believed to be a mixture of races that originally came from Asia and Micronesia (islands in the South Pacific). When these groups of people migrated to Japan, they brought valuable skills such as tool making with them. The descendants of the early Japanese learned about architecture, government, written language, and Buddhism from the Chinese who came to Japan later on. A unique culture emerged as the Japanese altered what they learned from others to suit their own way of life.

## Clans and emperors
Japan's civilization is thousands of years old. In the early days clans ruled sections of the country. Clans were large, powerful families that fought against one another for land and power. In the fourth century the leader of the Yamato clan became emperor. He claimed to be a descendant of Jinmu Tenno, who was believed to have descended from the sun goddess, Amaterasu. *Tenno,* which means "heavenly king," became the emperor's title. All the Japanese emperors can trace their family line back to Jinmu Tenno.

*A sculpture of Minamoto Yoritomo, Japan's first shogun.*

## The emperor's general
Emperors have reigned over Japan for over 1300 years. The emperor was not always the most powerful person in the land, however. The real power often belonged to military clans. In 1192 a man named Minamoto Yoritomo took control and ruled over all the clans. He was called *shogun. Shogun* means the "emperor's general." This powerful man made all the laws on behalf of the emperor and was obeyed by everyone without question.

## Feuding feudal lords
*Daimyo* were feudal lords. Each *daimyo* controlled an area of Japan, and the *shogun* ruled over the *daimyo.* The *samurai,* meaning "ones who serve," were the soldiers of the *daimyo.* The *daimyo* and their *samurai* often tried to win more land and power by fighting against other *daimyo.* For protection, the castle of a *daimyo* was surrounded by a moat and located on high ground.

## Japanese knights
The *samurai* were similar to the knights of medieval Europe. A *samurai's* armor was made of metal plates held together by colorful cords. His weapons were the bow and arrow, a curved dagger, and a long steel sword. Just as the medieval knights followed a code of honor, the *samurai* lived by "The Code of the Warriors," called *bushido. Bushido* instructed them in religion and martial arts, and taught them about loyalty, self-control, and noble behavior. The *samurai* believed that loyalty to their lord was the most important quality that a soldier could possess.

*(right) A **samurai** statue guards the entrance to an old **shogun** palace. A sword, dagger, bow, and arrows, were traditional **samurai** weapons.*

## A privileged class

At one time the *samurai* were the only people who rode horses, carried swords, and used last names. All these things were restricted to those who were thought to be of noble birth. Only a small portion of the population of Japan belonged to the privileged *samurai* class. The rest of society was made up of farmers, artisans, merchants, priests, and monks. Although the *samurai* had many privileges, the merchants and artisans were often much wealthier.

## Sealed off from the world

For seven hundred years Japan was ruled by *shogun* and their *samurai*. About three hundred years ago the *shogun* made a law called the Isolation Decree. This law stopped the Japanese from having contact with the outside world. No one was allowed to travel outside Japan, and no foreigners were permitted to enter the country. The people in positions of power believed that the way to have a unified country was to make sure that only Japanese ways were learned.

## New ideas

In 1853 an American military officer named Commodore Perry arrived on Japan's shores with a fleet of steamships. He demanded that the *shogun* allow the Americans to trade with Japan. The Japanese were not strong enough to fight the invaders and were forced to open their ports to the outside world. This event marked the beginning of a number of major changes. Many new ideas flooded into the country. The Japanese soon learned about railways, factories, steam power, electricity, and hundreds of other inventions.

Fifteen years later the ruling *shogun* was forced to resign, and Emperor Meiji gained power. Less than a hundred years later, after World War II, Japan became a democracy. Today Japan is governed by a group of elected representatives called the *Diet*. The head of the government is the Prime Minister. Although there is still an emperor, his position is ceremonial, similar to that of Great Britain's queen.

# What is your samurai-Q?

I.Q. is short for "intelligence quotient." It is one way of trying to assess a person's level of intelligence. Here is a fun test you can take to find out your Samurai-Q (pronounced samur-I.Q.).

How much do you know about samurai life? If you know very little, how well can you guess? Choose what you think the answer is for each question, and write it down on a piece of paper. Give yourself one point for each correct answer.

1. The word samurai means: a) one who fights b) one who serves c) one who rides a horse

2. A favorite samurai game was: a) *go* b) Chinese checkers c) marbles

3. At the age of seven a samurai boy received: a) wide trousers b) a sword c) a birthday cake

4. At the age of fifteen a samurai boy received: a) a sword b) a haircut c) both a and b

5. Before going to war, samurai warriors ate three lucky foods. These were: a) rice, fish, miso soup b) mashed potatoes, pickles, jellybeans c) shellfish, seaweed, chestnuts

6. The samurai hairstyle was: a) short spikes b) bald in front, ponytail in back c) bald all over

7. A samurai warrior sometimes did this before battle: a) brush his teeth b) blacken his teeth c) make a will

8. After battle, a samurai warrior enjoyed: a) sumo wrestling b) a nap c) the tea ceremony

9. Samurai armor was difficult to wear because: a) the cords tying the metal plates together got heavy when it rained b) the cords froze when it snowed c) the cords were often full of lice and ants d) all of the above

10. Samurai compared themselves to: a) cherry blossoms b) horses c) the sun

**Answers**: 1. b; 2. a. *Go* is a game of strategy in which one player captures another's pieces; 3. a. *Hakama* are wide trousers that were worn by the samurai; 4. c; 5. c; 6. b; 7. b; 8. c. The tea ceremony, a slow, ritualistic way of drinking tea, relaxed the samurai after battle; 9. d; 10. a. The samurai felt that their lives were as fragile and short as those of cherry blossoms.

*Those who belonged to the powerful **samurai** class wore elaborate costumes and rode horses. Sometimes **samurai** women fought alongside their husbands.*

*(opposite page, bottom) Adult **samurai** shaved only the front part of their heads; **samurai** boys shaved their heads all over, except for bangs and a topknot.*

## What is your Samurai-Q?

**9-10 points:** You are ready to be "one who serves."

**7-8 points:** You deserve a pair of *hakama*, or wide trousers.

**5-6 points:** You deserve a cup of green tea.

**3-4 points:** Put your hair into a ponytail and "think samurai."

**0-2 points:** Eat more chestnuts to improve your luck!

Not all of Japan is crowded. Small farming communities lie nestled in lush mountain valleys. Quiet fishing villages are scattered throughout the smaller islands. Although only a small number of Japanese live in these areas, they manage to provide the rest of the country with most of its food supply!

## A big job for a few farmers

Until this century more than half of all Japanese farmed for a living. Now only eight percent work to feed the rest of the population. More and more farm children are deciding not to stay on their parents' farms. They choose to work and live permanently in cities. Many farmers work at other jobs in nearby cities and spend only part of the day working on the land. They are able to do this because of new farm machines and because the other members of their families do most of the field work. Today much of the work on part-time farms is carried out by farming women and elders.

## Small, efficient farms

Japan's farms are small compared to those in other countries. The average-sized North American farm is more than one hundred times as big as the average Japanese farm. It is not unusual to find crops planted on tiny plots right in the middle of a Japanese city. Japan manages to produce three quarters of its own food because its small farms are efficiently operated.

## Winding terraces

Japan is famous for its evenly terraced farmlands that look like wide, winding stairs carved right into mountain slopes. Terraces enable farmers to use every bit of available land. Erosion is a big problem on terraced fields. These fields must be fertilized regularly to replace nutrients that have been washed away by storms and flooding.

*Evenly terraced farmlands enable farmers to use the land on mountain slopes to grow a variety of vegetables.*

## Changing crops

The diets of Japanese people have changed drastically over the past century. For a long, long time peasants grew rice for their lords but could not afford to eat rice themselves. They ate only barley, soya, millet, and pickled vegetables. When feudalism ended, everyone could afford rice, so it became the most important crop. In recent years, however, mixed farming has become important and takes up as much land as rice farming does. One third of Japan's land is used for growing rice, another third for tea, wheat, fruit, and vegetables; the remaining third is reserved for raising farm animals such as cattle, pigs, and chickens.

## Fishing

The Japanese catch and eat more fish than any other nation. In fact, they fish in every single ocean on earth! On average, Japanese citizens eat about forty-five kilograms of fish a year. By comparison, a person living in Europe or North America eats only five kilograms of fish in the same period of time.

## Three kinds of fishing

Fishing is a major industry in Japan. Three kinds of fishing are common: coastal fishing, fish farming, and deep-sea trawling. There are many fishing fleets as well as independent fishermen who harvest the coastal waters for such fish as sardine, tuna, and octopus.

## Fish farming

Aquaculture is a kind of "fish farming" that involves the breeding of fish in shallow waters along the coast. Yellow-tailed fish, shrimp, tuna, and oysters are examples of sea creatures that are farmed in this way. Fish-farming operations are usually run by families.

## Far out at sea

Some people work for large companies aboard huge fishing vessels. They live right on the ships and go on fishing voyages that last up to five months! These ships are like factories because they have the equipment to can and freeze their catch right on board. They provide fish for both home and foreign markets.

*The fishing boats in the harbor are colorfully decorated for one of Japan's many festivals.*

#  Rice farming

Hundreds of years ago the Japanese learned rice-growing techniques from the Chinese. Rice was used in so many different ways that it was considered to be more than just a valuable crop. The rice plant was originally believed to be a gift from the gods. For this reason the great ropes that hang in Shinto shrines are woven from rice straw. People also use rice straw to make sandals, hats, and *tatami* mats. As well as being a staple of the Japanese diet, rice grains are used to make a type of wine called *sake*.

## Two crops a year

Rice grows well in Japan's climate. Heavy rainfall, mild temperatures, and long hours of daylight allow farmers in many areas to grow two crops of rice each year. As a result, the Japanese are able to grow more rice on an area of farmland than the people of any other Asian rice-growing country!

## How rice is grown

Growing rice is a difficult process with many steps. Farmers used to do all the work by hand, but now almost everything is done by machine. At the beginning of the growing season farmers plant rice seeds in small plots of dry land. While the seeds are sprouting, they prepare wet fields, or paddies, for later.

## Flooding the fields

Rice needs plenty of water. Low walls of earth are built around sections of each paddy. Through a system of pipes, the paddies are flooded with water from nearby rivers. The walls, or dikes, separating the paddy sections prevent the water from running off.

## Snorkles on rice plants

Rice plants need oxygen to live, just as you do! Then how do they survive under water? With snorkles! Their leaves make tiny passageways by curling themselves into tubes. These tubes feed the roots with air from above the water line.

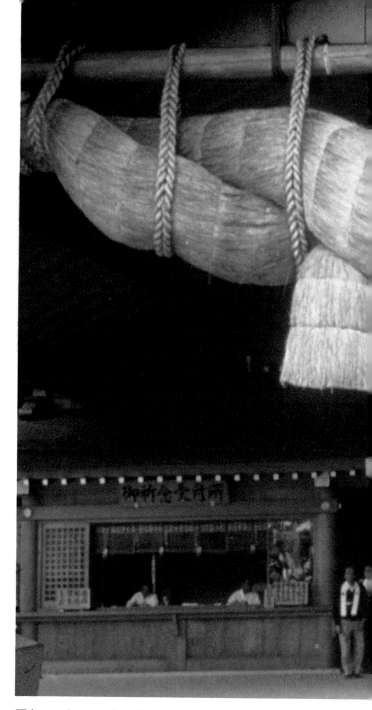

*This massive rope hanging at the entrance of a Shinto shrine is made of rice straw. The people beneath look tiny by comparison.*

## Transplanting

After three or four weeks the seeds in the dry fields have grown into small plants about twenty centimeters high. At this point they are ready to be transplanted into the wet paddies. Transplanting and tending rice plants used to be a difficult job that required a lot of bending. Family members, young and old, helped out. Paddy workers tucked up their pant legs and waded in barefoot. Today, on most farms, transplanting is done by machine.

*Machines are used to plant seedlings in flooded paddies. In the old days they were planted by hand.*

*Fully grown rice plants are cut down by a harvesting machine. Why is this crop so close to the buildings?*

## Harvest time

When the stalks of the plants are golden yellow, the rice is ready to be harvested. Farmers open the dikes and drain the water from the paddies. After the fields have dried, the rice is cut down by harvesting machines. In some areas the harvest season is very wet, so the rice plants cannot be laid on the ground to dry. Instead, the farmers hang the plants from elevated frames. Each village or region has its own special style of bundling and hanging the rice to dry.

## Threshing

When you think of rice, you probably think of the tiny white or brown grains that you buy in bags. These are only a small part of the rice plant. Rice grains must be removed from the plant by hitting or striking it. This process, called threshing, is either done by hand or machine. The rice grains are put in sacks and transported to factories where the shell around each grain is removed. The rice is then packaged and shipped to stores.

In the past getting from place to place in Japan was very difficult. Steep mountains made journeys dangerous and time-consuming. Traveling by river was next to impossible because most of Japan's rivers are short, rocky rapids tumbling out of mountain sides.

## Tunnels and bridges

Today long tunnels through mountains and huge bridges over river valleys make traveling a lot less difficult. The Japanese have also built water-tight tunnels beneath the sea. Undersea tunnels connect the islands of Honshu, Kyushu, and Hokkaido. The tunnel to Hokkaido is almost fifty-four kilometers long, making it the longest underwater tunnel in the world. The tunnels and bridges among the islands service both cars and trains. Some trains run along elevated tracks above streets, whereas others run underground in subways.

## Public transportation

Although many Japanese people own cars, there is very little space for parking. Most people use their cars only on weekends. They use public transportation during the week.

Japan has one of the most sophisticated public transportation systems in the world. Thousands of people spend up to four hours a day going to and from work on commuter trains. The train is such a popular mode of transportation that it is usually crowded, and the majority of passengers must stand the whole way. At some subway stations in Tokyo professional "pushers" are employed to cram people into the train during rush hours. It is necessary to shove passengers aboard because the train does not start until the doors are properly shut.

*The Seto Ohashi, the bridge to Shikoku, is the last link joining Japan's four main islands.*

*The "bullet train," or* shinkansen, *is now the fastest train on earth. The maglev will soon surpass the* shinkansen *for comfort, silence, and speed!*

## As fast as a speeding bullet!

You are waiting on a crowded platform for the speedy *shinkansen*. Lines are marked on the platform to let you know exactly where the doors will open. At its scheduled arrival time—in precisely fifteen seconds—the train will pull into the station. You hop aboard and, within minutes, you are traveling at speeds of over two hundred kilometers per hour. A main computer in Tokyo controls all 150 trains as they speed in and out of the major cities every few minutes. The *shinkansen* is the quickest and most reliable way to travel in Japan.

## Faster still!

In the very near future the Japanese hope to be whisking train passengers along at speeds of over five hundred kilometers per hour. Japanese engineers are working to perfect an entirely new type of train known as maglev, which is short for "magnetically levitated." The maglev is a vehicle without wheels that looks like a cross between a *shinkansen* and a spacecraft. It is built to provide a truly comfortable ride. Because the maglev will hover about ten centimeters above its track, its passengers will never feel the clickety-clack of wheels vibrating against the rails!

## How does it work?

The maglev and its walled track are both fitted with metal coils. These coils become magnetized when an electric current is passed through them. The magnets on the track and the train alternately attract and repel each other. Controlled by a computer, this finely adjusted system of electromagnets will keep the train moving straight and at the right distance above the track. Maglev is designed to be so fast that it might someday replace airplanes for overland travel.

*Even though Japan has an efficient public transit system, subway platforms become very crowded during rush hours because there are millions of commuters.*

For centuries the majority of Japanese were rice farmers. Cultivating rice in the old days was back-breaking work. Peasants toiled long hours to feed themselves and their families. This tradition of hard work has been passed on to the modern industrial Japanese.

The fact that Japan has very few raw materials has not stopped the Japanese from producing a multitude of manufactured goods. More products in electronics, computers, cars, steel, industrial machinery, and plastics are made in Japan than in any other country.

## Automobiles

Since 1980 Japan has led the world in the production of automobiles. In the future, however, the industry may not be as profitable as it once was. Other countries are buying fewer Japanese cars and are now producing more vehicles at their own automobile plants. Japanese cars are also becoming more expensive because Japanese autoworkers are paid higher wages than autoworkers in other countries.

## Shipbuilding

Since Japan is an island nation, it is not surprising that shipbuilding is one of its major industries. Oil rigs, supertankers, ferryboats, and ships with energy-saving, computer-controlled sails are just a few examples of Japan's ocean-going vessels.

*This robot is playing the organ, but most robots are used in industry. An industrial robot never gets tired of doing the same tasks and always produces a good product.*

## Micro-chips

Today's computers are fast, efficient, and can store huge amounts of information. Without micro-chips, computers would not be as small and advanced as they are now. Micro-chips are the "brains" that operate computers and other high-tech products. They are paper-thin electronic circuits that contain a computer's memory and operating functions. For over twenty years the Japanese have been developing ways to make smaller and more powerful chips. Thanks to these tiny chips, Japan is able to produce high-resolution television sets, lightweight video cameras, compact stereos, and the world's best robots!

## Amazing the world with robots

Since the late 1960s Japan has been responsible for some of the world's most ingenious robots. The Japanese have produced two-legged robots that can walk, seeing-eye robots to aid the blind, and robots that wait on customers in restaurants. Robots have been programmed to perform thousands of amazing feats.

The Japanese have invented many sophisticated industrial robots for use on factory assembly lines. (See picture on page 26.) Robots help increase production. They perform numerous tasks that people find boring and meaningless. They can also be used to carry out such dangerous jobs as handling toxic chemicals.

## The Little Giant

Today Japan is sometimes called the "Little Giant" because, although it is small, it is a very powerful country. Japan became industrialized in half the time it took other nations to do so. The Japanese have improved their standard of living through determination, hard work, and cooperation.

*Japan is a leading international trader. The stock market located in Tokyo is the largest in the world.*

# ✳ Industry, pollution, and recycling ✳

Many kinds of pollution have occurred as a result of Japan's rapid industrial growth. Between 1950 and 1970 Japan did not put much thought or effort into pollution control. In every big city, factories spewed smoke into the air and dumped toxic waste into the water.

Soon people in contaminated areas began to suffer from pollution-related diseases. Many of these diseases are now known around the world by Japanese names because they were first identified in Japan. For instance, metals such as mercury and cadmium found their way into the food chain. The disease caused by mercury poisoning is known worldwide as *minimata*,

and cadmium causes the disease *itai-itai*. *Itai-itai* means "It hurts, it hurts" in Japanese. People with these diseases suffer severe pain, brain disorders, brittle bones, and birth defects.

## Pollution controls

As people became more concerned about the environment, they sought solutions to industrial-waste problems. In the 1970s the Japanese government passed laws to control the huge amounts of toxic waste that industries were dumping into the air and water and onto the land. Industries were forced to develop pollution-control devices that filtered out many of the harmful substances they produced.

*Garbage trucks take waste to a local recycling depot.*

These controls have helped but not solved Japan's pollution problems. Regulations and devices help prevent some pollution from entering the environment, but they do nothing about pollution that already exists. Pollution that is taken out of the air, for example, still remains as polluted dust on the land. Scientists and engineers from many countries are working toward reducing the dangers of industrial waste.

## Recycling champions

People all over the world are finding it more and more difficult to know what to do with their garbage. In Japan people sort all their garbage according to the materials it contains, such as glass, tin, and paper. There are weekly schedules for garbage pickups. In many cities different types of waste are collected at specific times on certain days. The second Tuesday in the month, for instance, might be the day to put out batteries.

Much of Japan's household garbage is turned into useful products. The rest is taken to dumps where it is inspected for dangerous substances and then burned in large incinerators. The ash from the incinerated trash is also checked to make sure it can be dumped safely into landfill sites. No other country can claim to manage its garbage as carefully as Japan does. The Japanese are recycling champions!

*(above left) Industries such as car plants pollute the air and water around them.*

27

There is not much flat land in Japan, so most of Japan's major cities are crowded along the coast of Honshu island. Japan's biggest cities are Tokyo, Osaka, Yokohama, and Nagoya.

## Tokyo, the huge capital

Tokyo, the capital, is the largest and most crowded city of all. It is one of the most densely populated areas of the world. This giant metropolis is made up of twenty-six smaller cities as well as fifteen towns and villages. Tokyo holds one tenth of Japan's entire population, making it home to almost twelve million people.

If you were to live in a city such as Tokyo, you would have to be an expert at finding your way through a maze of concrete-and-steel buildings and up and down many levels of underground shopping malls. You could visit the *Ginza*, the famous Japanese shopping district, or *Akihabara* where shops have the latest Japanese electrical goods on display. You can find a perfect place for an afternoon picnic at the Imperial Palace gardens. In Tokyo you can also hear music played by international rock groups, watch a traditional *kabuki* play, or enjoy a day at Tokyo's Disneyland. To live in a Japanese city is to be part of a fascinating and busy lifestyle.

*A peaceful park on the outskirts of the ancient city of Kyoto*

## Kyoto, heart of Japan

If there is one city that all Japanese people want to visit, it is the city of Kyoto. Fifty million tourists from all over make the trip each year. What is the reason? Kyoto is the best place to see the peaceful images of ancient Japan: women in fancy kimonos, tea houses in secluded gardens, and tall *pagodas* outlined against the sky. Even though a million-and-a-half people live there now, it is still possible to find the wooden houses and narrow lanes of the past, just behind the busy modern streets. In the tree-covered mountains that surround the city are nestled two thousand temples and shrines.

## Coping with crowds

Almost three quarters of Japan's people live in congested cities. How do people cope with being in such small spaces with so many other people? The answer is good manners. When the Japanese are tightly packed in groups, such as when they are waiting for a subway train, they do not push and shove. Most people patiently wait their turn. The Japanese also make the best of cramped office and living space. Furniture and belongings are carefully organized in order to make rooms look more spacious. For example, by adjusting the furniture at night, a living room can become a bedroom.

# Japanese ways...

Match the pictures with the descriptions below. If you want to learn more about the people and culture of Japan, read *Japan: the People* and *Japan: the Culture*.

## Headbands

Headbands, or *hachimaki*, are worn to show that a person is preparing for a big mental, physical, or spiritual challenge. The *samurai* wore headbands under their helmets during battle. Today Japanese people wear them on many different occasions such as at festivals or during exam preparation.

## Rub-a-dub dub

To the Japanese, bathing is not just for getting clean. It is a relaxing pastime to be shared with family and friends. These Japanese children are sharing one big bath at a day-care center as part of their daily routine.

## Making use of roof tops

In Japan, where space is precious, roof tops serve as volleyball courts, public gardens, and even as amusement parks complete with rides. Department stores have pleasant roof-top gardens where shoppers can relax while their children play games.

## Disneyland in Tokyo?

You might think you are looking at a picture of Disneyland in California, but actually, you are seeing the Sleeping Beauty Castle at Tokyo's Disneyland. In every detail this Disneyland is a replica of the original. The Japanese are such passionate Mickey Mouse fans that they even have Mickey stores and Mickey hotels!

## Yoyogi Park

It is Sunday in Yoyogi Park and seven teenagers dressed in black clothes are performing their much-rehearsed dance routine to the song "Rock Around the Clock." Every Sunday many groups of young people gather in this Tokyo park dressed in costumes from the 1950s.

# Glossary

**adapt** - To adjust for a different situation; to make suitable

**ancestors** - People from whom one is descended

**artisan** - A craftsperson or skilled worker

**cadmium** - A soft, bluish white metal that is mixed with other metals to create strong surfaces. It is dangerous to people's health.

**ceremonial** - Characterized by a set of formal customs performed for a particular occasion

**clan** - A group of families that claims to have the same ancestors

**commuter train**- A train on which people travel long distances to work

**coastline** - The boundary between land and sea

**culture** - The customs, beliefs, and arts of a distinct group of people

**democracy** - A form of government in which people elect representatives to make decisions for society

**descendants** - People who come from a particular family blood line

**earth's crust** - The surface layer of the earth

**erosion** - The gradual washing away of soil and rocks by rain, wind, or running water

**feudalism** - A class system based on the relationship between lords and the people who pledge services to these lords

**invader** - Someone who enters by force

*kabuki* - A type of Japanese theatrical production

**landslide** - Rock or soil falling down a hillside or mountainside

**martial art** - A sport that uses warlike techniques for the purposes of self-defense and exercise

**medieval** - Something that occurred during the Middle Ages (500-1500 A.D.)

**metropolis** - A large city made up of many smaller cities

**millet** - A type of grain

*miso* - Wheat, rice, or soybean paste to which water, salt, seaweed, and vegetables are added to make a soup

**natural phenomenon** - A remarkable happening in nature that can either be seen, heard, felt, smelled or tasted. Earthquakes and quicksand are examples of natural phenomena.

**original people** - The people who lived in an area before any other people

**paddy** - A rice field

*pagoda* - A type of building that looks like several one-story buildings stacked one on top of another

**raw material** - A substance from the earth that is not yet processed or refined

**replica** - An exact copy of an original item

**ritual** - A formal custom in which several steps are faithfully followed

*tatami* - A standard-sized mat woven from rice straw

**toxic** - Poisonous

**trawling** - A way of fishing by dragging a strong net, shaped like a bag, along the ocean floor

**tremor** - A shaking or quivering of the ground

# Index

56789 WP Printed in the U.S.A. 87654